The bracelet

Contents

The bracelet

Kamala sat by the pond in her garden.
The sun was shining and the birds
were singing. It had been a busy
day and now Kamala just wanted to be quiet.
She opened her book and started to read.

Suddenly, the birds stopped singing.
Kamala looked up and saw a magpie on
the grass in front of her. There was a
bracelet by its feet. The bracelet was
shining in the sun.

The magpie looked at Kamala and then it
opened its mouth and said,
"This is for you but not just for you,
so that you can do what you have to do."
It looked at her for a while and then it flew off.

6

Kamala was very surprised. She picked up the bracelet and looked at it. It had three stones in it: a red stone, a blue stone and a green one. They were shining in the sun.

What was it the magpie had said?
"This is for you but not just for you,
so that you can do what you have to do."

It was very strange! Kamala put the bracelet on her
arm. She looked at it and then said to herself,
"It's lovely."

The next morning, Kamala set off for school.
She saw Vijay in front of her. He was her
friend Panna's little brother. Vijay was
eating some crisps. Suddenly, a big boy
jumped out in front of him.

"Give me your crisps," the boy said to Vijay.

"No, they're mine," Vijay said.

"Oh no they aren't; they're mine now. Give them to me," said the boy and he grabbed Vijay's arm.

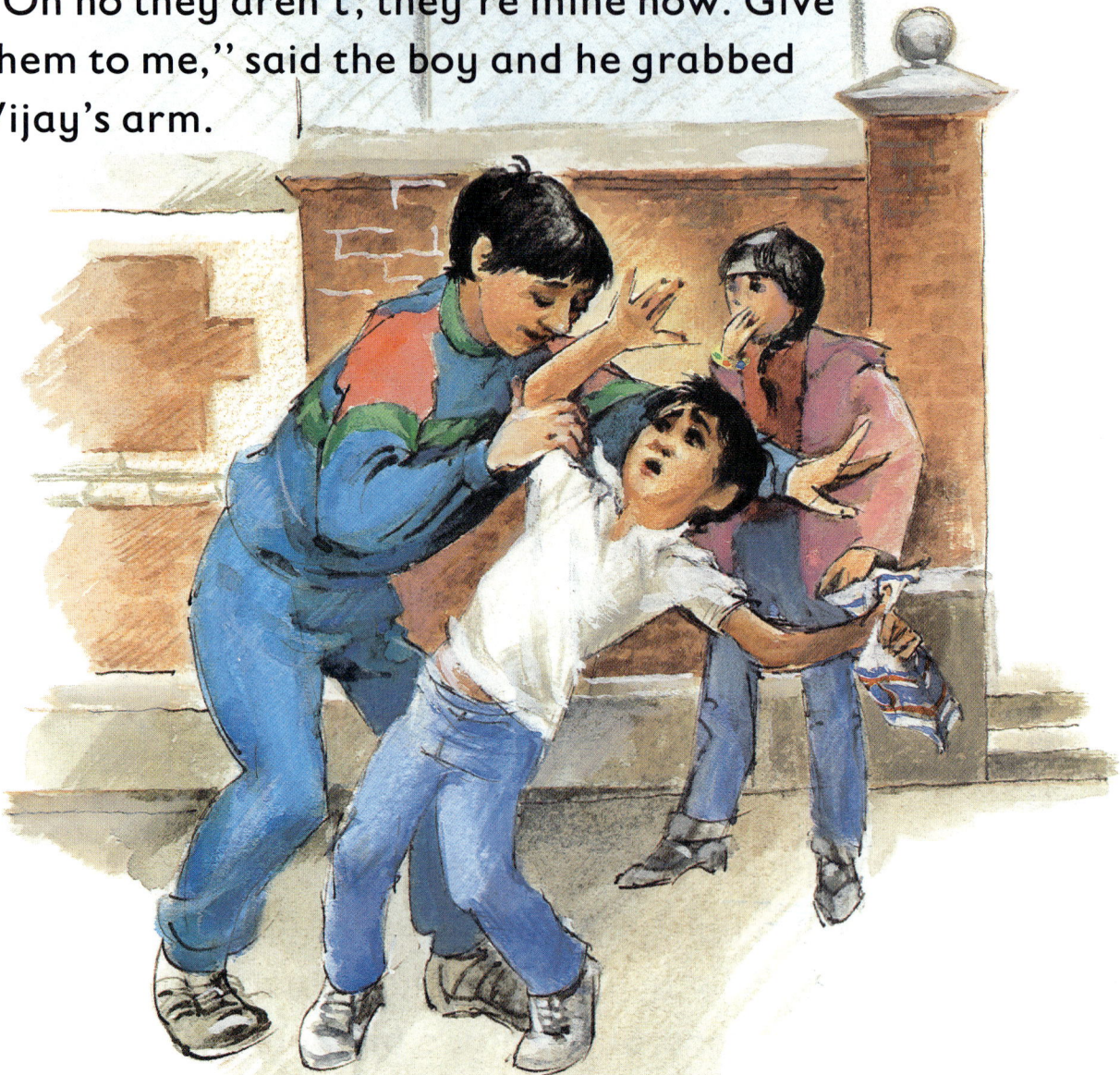

"Leave him alone!" shouted Kamala.

The big boy looked at her and then he said,
"You keep your nose out of this. I want
those crisps and I'm going to have them.
You can't stop me, so there!"

Kamala turned to Vijay. He was looking very scared. What was she going to do now? How could she make the boy leave Vijay alone? Kamala didn't know what to do. She started to play with the bracelet on her arm.

She touched the red stone. Suddenly, something very strange happened. The bracelet started to get bigger! Kamala took it off. The bracelet was getting bigger all the time. Now she knew what to do!

Kamala threw the bracelet over the boy's head.
It dropped down and trapped his arms.
"Aaah!" he yelled. He couldn't move!
The boy was very surprised. So was Vijay!

"Go on, Vijay," Kamala said, "you get off to
school. I'll look after him."
Vijay walked away. He didn't understand what
had happened but he liked what
Kamala had done!

"Right," Kamala said to the boy. "If I let you go will you promise never to do that again?"

The boy felt scared. Who could tell what this girl might do next! So he said,
"Let me go, I promise I won't do it again."

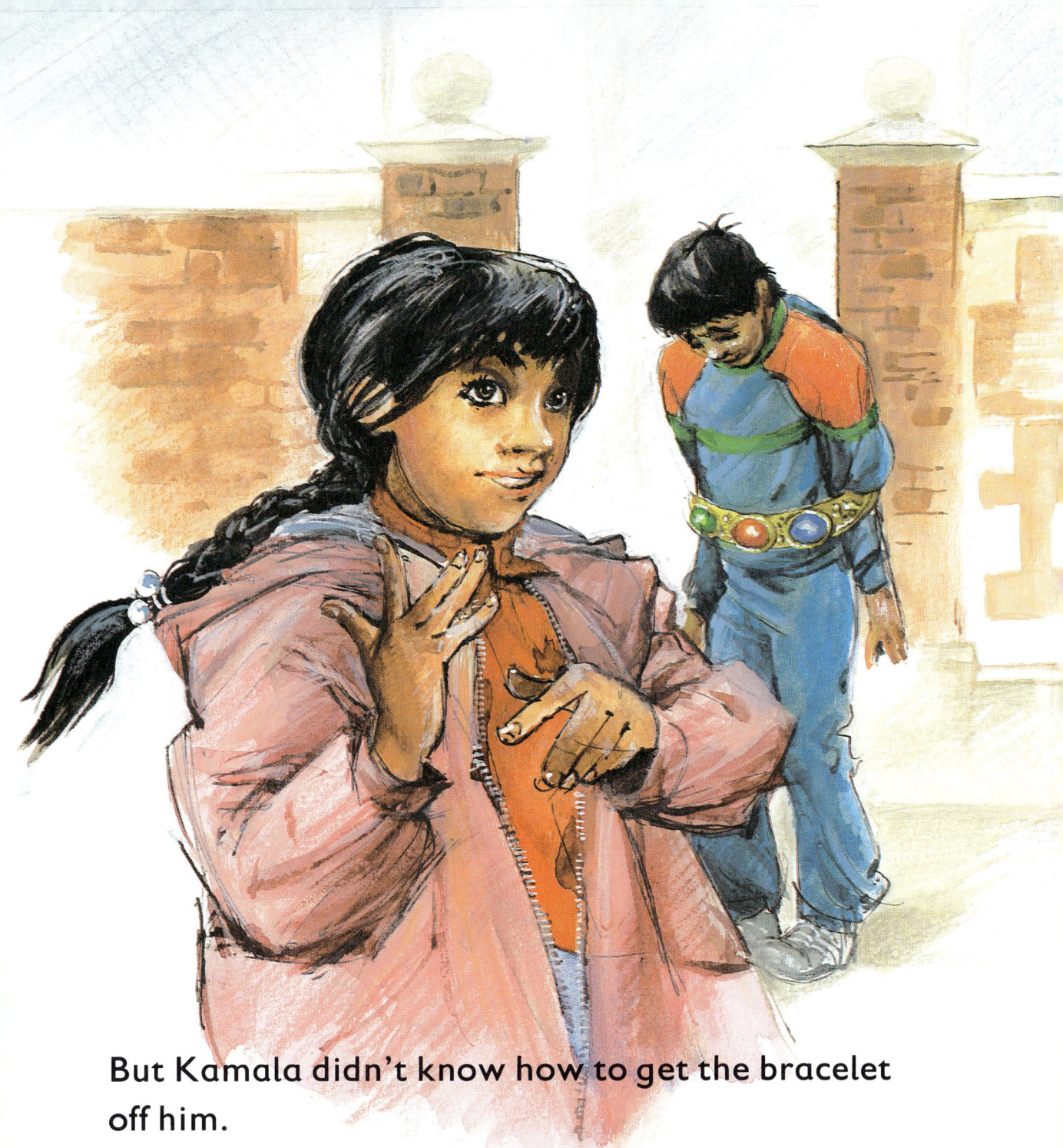

But Kamala didn't know how to get the bracelet
off him.
"Perhaps if I just tell it to come back to
me, it will," she thought. "I hope so."

"Come back, bracelet," Kamala said.
The bracelet came off the boy and flew over to
Kamala. It was small again by the time
she caught it. She put it on and
then she looked at the boy.

"Right, off you go," she said to him.
"And you just remember your promise. I'll be after you if you don't."
The boy ran off. He couldn't wait to get away from this funny girl and her bracelet!

Kamala looked at the bracelet on her arm.
She knew now that it must be a magic one.
It got bigger when she touched the red stone.
What would it do if she touched the green or the
blue one?
"I must find out," she said to herself.

Kamala touched the green stone.
"That's funny," she said. "Nothing's happened."
Then she saw her friend Panna coming down
the street. Kamala waited for her and then she
said, "Hello."

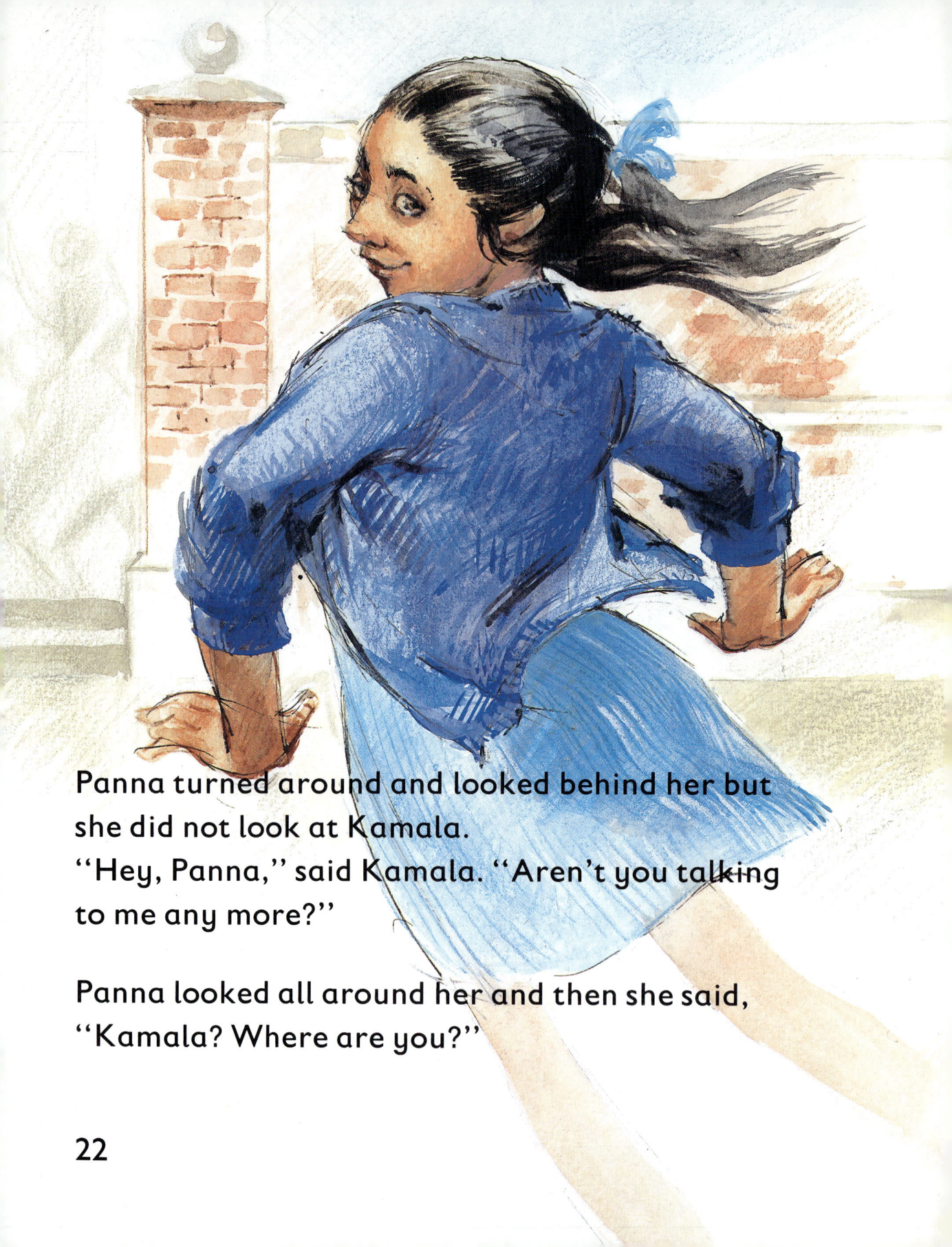

Panna turned around and looked behind her but
she did not look at Kamala.
"Hey, Panna," said Kamala. "Aren't you talking
to me any more?"

Panna looked all around her and then she said,
"Kamala? Where are you?"

"I'm right in front of you. Stop messing about!"
Kamala said. Then she knew what had happened.
Panna wasn't messing about. She couldn't see
Kamala because Kamala was invisible!

Kamala laughed and then she touched the blue stone. "Here I am," she said.

"I don't understand, where were you?" asked Panna.

So Kamala told her everything that had happened. Then she said, "Having this bracelet is going to be fun, isn't it?"

Who's there?

Kamala and Panna were in Kamala's bedroom.
Panna did not look very happy.
"What's wrong?" Kamala asked her.

"Nothing," Panna answered.

"Yes, there is," said Kamala. "Tell me what's wrong."

"Well," said Panna. "You know that painting
I did at school today?"

"Yes," answered Kamala. "I know, the one with
the dragon eating the witch."

"That's it," said Panna. "Well, I was on my way home when Susan came up to me. She grabbed my painting and tore it all up. Then she pulled my hair and ran away laughing."

"That's just the kind of thing she would do,"
said Kamala. "She's horrible. Nobody likes her."

"Yes, but what can we do about it?" asked Panna.

"Leave it to me," said Kamala. "I know how we
can stop her being so horrible . . ."

At school the next day, Kamala and Panna were doing some painting. Susan was at a table all by herself. She was painting, too. Kamala looked around the room. Everyone was busy. "I'll do it now," she said to Panna.

Kamala went and asked the teacher if she could go out. Then, as soon as she was outside the door, she touched her bracelet. This time, it was the green stone that she touched. Soon there was no Kamala. She was invisible again.

Kamala went back into the room. Nobody could
see her because she was invisible. She went over
to Susan's table and she pulled her hair.
"Ow!" yelled Susan.

"What's wrong with you, Susan?" the teacher asked.

"Someone pulled my hair," Susan answered.

"Don't be silly, Susan, there's nobody near you," the teacher said. "Stop making things up and get on with your painting."

Susan was cross. She turned round and pulled a
face at Panna. But while Susan wasn't looking,
Kamala did something. She painted a ghost on
Susan's piece of paper.

"Aaah!" yelled Susan.

"Now what's wrong with you, Susan?" asked
the teacher.

"Someone painted a ghost on my piece of paper,"
Susan answered.

But the teacher said,
"Don't be silly, Susan, there's nobody near you.
Stop making things up and get on with your painting."

Susan wasn't cross now. She was scared.
What was going on? She looked around the room.
Who was doing this to her?

She looked back at her painting and her mouth dropped open. Kamala had painted something next to the ghost . . .

Now Susan was very scared. There was nobody near her. Who was painting on her piece of paper? She was just going to yell again when her pencil moved. It started to write . . .

I promise
I'll never be horrible
to anyone ever
again.

Susan

Kamala put the pencil down and Susan
yelled again.
"What is it this time, Susan?" asked the teacher.
She went over to Susan's table. She looked at
the paper and then she looked at Susan.

"I understand, Susan," she said. "This is your way of telling everyone that you are sorry for all the bad things you have done.
Good girl. I'm pleased with you."

Then the teacher said to everyone,
"Susan has something to tell you all.
Read it out, Susan."
Susan didn't know what to do.

So she looked around at everyone and then
she said quietly,
"I promise I'll never be horrible to anyone ever again."
Then something pulled her hair and so she said,
"I'm sorry for what I've done and I'm sorry
for what I did to you, Panna."

"Good for you," someone said in her ear.
"And you just remember what you said if you
don't want the ghost to get you!"
Then Kamala went out of the room and
touched the blue stone on her bracelet.

Kamala went and sat down again.
Then she said to Panna,
"I still don't know where that magpie came
from or why it let me have the bracelet.
But it's a lot of fun all the same!"

How could Kamala use her bracelet here?

Ask me a riddle

What do you give a sick bird?

Tweetment.

Why do birds fly south in the winter?

Because it's too far to walk.

What's black and white and red all over?

A sun-burned penguin.

What goes "Quick – quick"?

A duck with hiccups.

What goes, "Ha ha bonk"?

A worm laughing its head off.

What did the duck say at Christmas?

"I'm a Christmas quacker."